Alice was beginning to get very tired of sitting by her sister on the bank, and of having nothing to do: once or twice she peeped into the book her sister was reading, but it had no pictures or conversations in it, "and what is the use of a book," thought Alice, "without pictures or conversations?"

Lewis Carroll *Alice's Adventures in Wonderland*

A picture book is a drama. We aim to lead the eye to the bit of the stage where the main action is taking place, to highlight a telling gesture, a touching facial expression or an important detail tucked away somewhere which is a vital clue to the plot. And, more importantly, to invite the reader to inhabit that interface between word and image, the space you are always trying to leave for their own imagination.

Shirley Hughes *A Life Drawing*

Introduction

The Kate Greenaway Medal was established by The Library Association in 1955 for distinguished illustration in a book for children and young people. It is widely held to be the United Kingdom's most prestigious award for children's book illustration. The Medal is named after the popular nineteenth-century artist who, along with her contemporaries, Walter Crane and Randolph Caldecott, was known and respected for producing best-selling children's illustrations and designs.

The Medal was not presented in its inaugural year, as no book was considered suitable, but was first presented to Edward Ardizzone for *Tim All Alone*. It was a popular choice. The author Eleanor Farjeon wrote in a letter to the Youth Libraries Group: "One of my greatest happinesses has been hearing of the award of the Kate Greenaway Medal which has been bestowed on dear Ted Ardizzone." He had illustrated her book, *The Little Book Room,* which had won the Carnegie Medal the year before; she goes on to say, "I'm sure he did my job by proxy last year with an aplomb I could never have achieved".

In 2007, the Kate Greenaway Medal celebrates its Golden Jubilee. Over the past fifty years, it has recognised some of the very best illustrated books for children and young people and rewarded their illustrators with the much sought-after gold medal. It is, to use the words of twice-winner Michael Foreman, "the one they most want to win". What makes the Kate Greenaway Medal special is its unique judging process which is firmly rooted in the professional knowledge and experience of children's librarians. While other awards rely on media hype or publisher submissions, the books submitted for the Kate Greenaway Medal have been read and nominated by librarians who are committed to quality in children's books and who work daily with young readers.

All categories of illustrated books for children originally published in English in the United Kingdom are eligible for the Medal. Most of the winning books have been picture books, although five non-fiction books, three illustrated novels and a poetry collection have quite rightly been recognized.

The subjects, themes and formats of the winning books have been richly varied. There are Greek myths, English legends, traditional fairytales, a collection of nursery rhymes and a pop-up book. There are pen and ink drawings, delicate watercolours, oil paintings, collages and computer-generated images. There are stories about wolves, pirates, immigrant families and a runaway child living on the streets, to name just a few.

What links all these books over the fifty years of the awards is the sheer quality of their illustration and design. They have all been judged against criteria that have developed over the years, but which have always focused on excellence in terms of artistic style, format, synergy between the text and illustration, and the overall impact of the book on its reader. Put simply, the book that wins the Kate Greenaway Medal "should be a book of outstanding artistic quality; the whole work should provide pleasure from a stimulating and satisfying visual experience".

In this celebratory publication, we have chosen an image from each Medal-winning book which we think demonstrates its outstanding artistic quality and have written a brief commentary to explain why we think this is the case. Obviously we cannot do justice to an entire book in this way, but we hope it will provide a glimpse into the many wonderful books and talented illustrators that have been awarded the Medal in its fifty-year history. Writing this book has given us the opportunity to re-discover and review the work of favourite, and sometimes long-forgotten, illustrators. We hope that it provides you with that opportunity too.

Ian Dodds and Sue Roe

July 2007

1956

Edward Ardizzone
Tim All Alone

It is fitting that an artist often cited by other illustrators as a major influence on their work should have been the first recipient of the Kate Greenaway Medal. Edward Ardizzone received the award for *Tim All Alone*, one of a series of books published between 1936 and 1972 featuring the seafaring adventures of a resourceful young hero. The story of a boy who returns home to find his parents missing and then sets off on a long sea journey to find them, may seem unlikely to a modern audience, but its theme is a common one in children's literature.

A delicate and detailed use of pen, ink and watercolour is combined with the artist's characteristic use of intricate cross-hatching to achieve effects of light, shade and shape. Edward Ardizzone developed this style over time and honed it during his years as an official war artist. He described himself as a 'suggestive draughtsman': not wanting to draw things exactly as they are. His skill lies in using body language and posture to suggest mood and emotion in his characters: the views of Tim's bowed back poignantly express his sadness and despair. Colour is used subtly to emphasise this, for instance, the sea and sky change to grey when Tim's ship sails away without him. Hand-lettered speech balloons are used to great effect to further illuminate character and to move the plot forward.

The artist conveys a great deal with a few carefully-placed lines. The early illustration of Tim leaving Sea View looks very simple, but shows great control of line and perspective to achieve a sense of movement in the trees, clouds and sea. Edward Ardizzone's love of the sea and ships shine through the book and has its source in memories of his long sea voyage to England as a child and in the hours spent playing aboard the boats of Ipswich docks with his cousin. All the illustrations of the sea, with its changing wave shapes and colours, are atmospheric and the details of shipboard life are totally convincing.

Edward Ardizzone was regarded as Britain's most eminent children's book illustrator for much of the twentieth century with an international reputation and a uniquely recognisable style. In this book, his lively action drawings and delicate colour washes are combined with a real understanding of a child's longing for adventure and the pull of distant horizons.

Edward Ardizzone

Tim All Alone

Oxford University Press, 1956

Then he got up, turned his back on the house and set out on his way once more.

He was determined to search, if necessary, the whole wide world until he had found his parents.

1957

V H Drummond
Mrs Easter and the Storks

Violet Drummond's warmth and kindly humour shine through in this picture book, in which Mrs Easter and her nephew, Billie Guftie, set out on an adventure to reunite two devoted storks. Recognisable characters from the artist's earlier picture books, including the eccentric Mr Finch, Keeper of the King's Pets' Home, also make an appearance.

The illustrations are sketchily drawn in black ink. Simple line drawings are scattered throughout the text, while larger full-page illustrations are filled or overlaid with blocks of bright primary colour. Although only a restricted colour palette of red, blue and yellow has been used, the result is remarkably effective and brings life to the landscapes and views over the city. The city scenes are nicely composed and incredible detail has been put into the rooftops and chimney stacks.

Mrs Easter and the cast of sweetly grotesque supporting characters are all simply but humorously drawn. Visual clues are provided to Mrs Easter's no-nonsense personality, particularly the use of her trademark parasol, as she marches straight-backed through the city or proudly rides on the back of a flying stork. Body shapes and facial expressions are well realised with every eye and mouth line used to convey meaning and emotion.

The style and sequencing of the images in this book have a cartoon-like feeling to them, and it's interesting to note that Violet Drummond went on to design and produce a series of cartoons for the BBC.

V H Drummond
Mrs Easter and the Storks
Faber and Faber, 1957

1959

William Stobbs
Kashtanka

The precision of William Stobbs's drawings effectively and accurately illustrate Anton Chekhov's little-known Russian tale about a frightened dog who finds a new life in the home of a kindly circus performer.

Pages with black and white line drawings alternate with full-colour illustrations. Both are simply executed, although there is more detail in the clean, unbroken lines of the black and white drawings. The larger full page illustrations are filled with bright colour which capture the essence of old Russia and add to the almost fairytale or folkloric nature of the story. Period and place is conveyed in the background detail, including clothes, patterns on wallpaper and fabric, and the ornamental details of the buildings.

There is an interesting sense of design and perspective to all the illustrations. Objects like beds, tables, chairs and rugs appear to be squashed flat onto the page, giving the whole work an almost naïve style. Although the illustrations appear to lack vitality and movement, particularly as the animals perform their circus tricks, the artist does provide a sense of emotion and mood through some very simple touches: the dog's lolloping tongue; the cat's arched back; and the threateningly broad open wingspan of the goose.

William Stobbs was awarded the 1959 Kate Greenaway Medal jointly for *Kashtanka* and for his black and white line drawings in *A Bundle of Ballads*, a collection of old minstrels' ballads compiled by Ruth Manning-Sanders and published by Oxford University Press.

Anton Chekhov

Kashtanka

Illustrated by William Stobbs

Oxford University Press, 1959

1960

Gerald Rose
Old Winkle and the Seagulls

Gerald Rose's characteristic humour and lively illustrative style are evident in the story of Old Winkle, a fisherman whose knowledge of the seagulls' ways ends a fish shortage in his seaside town.

This is one of a number of picture books written and illustrated by husband and wife team Elizabeth and Gerald Rose in response to what they considered to be a dearth of good illustrations for children at the time.

The simple story of kindness rewarded is enhanced by Gerald Rose's illustrations which describe the quirky details of life in a seaside community. The illustrations are cartoon-like. The fisherman are particularly endearing characters with their woolly jumpers, bobble hats, boots and beards and single lines or mouth outlines conveying their mood.

Pages with black and white line illustrations alternate with full-colour pages and, occasionally, a border of colour with text alongside. The black and white illustrations are packed with amusing details to pore over: the fish leap energetically out of the sea into Old Winkle's net; the seagulls appear to be hovering on the wind to catch bread; and the fishmonger's cat changes from thin and sad to fat, happy and surrounded by fish bones. The colour illustrations are less detailed with broader strokes of paint and swirling shapes for the sea and sky, but they have their humour too, as in the picture of the Mayor's bald head which resembles the boiled egg he is forced to eat instead of a juicy kipper. The artist's greatest strength in his colour illustrations, however, is that by using a fairly muted palette he succeeds in matching the colour tones and movement of the sea, the shore and a sky full of hovering seagulls.

Elizabeth Rose
Old Winkle and the Seagulls
Illustrated by Gerald Rose
Faber and Faber, 1960

Immediately he threw his nets overboard and felt the weight of the fish as he hauled them in. Never had Winkle seen such a number as he drew them to the surface and filled his boat until it could hold no more.

1961

Antony Maitland
Mrs Cockle's Cat

Peter Cockle, the cat of the title, stares out boldly from his chimney-pot vantage point on the cover of this picture book; he is surrounded by the curling black letters which mirror his shape and capriciousness and emphasise his position as the most important character in the story. Mrs Cockle spends nearly all of her meagre wages as a balloon seller on fish for Peter, but when the fish runs out the ungrateful cat abandons her and they are only reunited when a gust of wind takes Mrs Cockle and her balloons on an amazing cloud-top journey to the seaside.

Antony Maitland is perhaps best known as an illustrator of novels and his skilful line drawing techniques are well suited to this text-heavy picture book. Black line illustrations with hatching and pastel shading share the page with, or shape around, blocks of text. Colour illustrations with a muted range of yellow, brown, blue and green appear at intervals, but, here too, the use of black line predominates. The illustrations have a strong sense of movement, particularly when depicting the weather, with trees bending and cloud shapes swirling in the wind. The use of viewpoint is interesting as it moves from an unusual title page, where Mrs Cockle and Peter appear to draw back the page to let the story begin, to the rooftop and aerial views at the end of the book.

The old-fashioned feel of this book is offset by touches of humour in its illustrations, chiefly in the character of Peter the cat with his intent way of staring at any fish to be found, even those he imagines in the flames of the fire.

Philippa Pearce

Mrs Cockle's Cat

Illustrated by Antony Maitland

Constable Young Books, 1961

Mrs. Cockle was naturally upset, but there was nothing to be done, so she went off to her street-corner as usual. She said to herself that the wilful cat would certainly be waiting outside the front door when she went home in the evening. She was only worried about what might happen to him in the meantime. Just suppose, Mrs. Cockle thought, he tried to sneak a piece of nice fresh fish from somebody's larder, and they set a dog after him? Or worse, supposing he tried to steal something from the fish shop, and a policeman caught him at it?

1962

Brian Wildsmith
ABC

Brian Wildsmith brings a startlingly uninhibited, painterly approach to this alphabet book of animals. From its bright red front cover with splashes of pink, turquoise and yellow paint, it is a feast of colliding colours and patterns. The depictions of the animals are a rich visual experience. Layers of colour have been stroked onto the paper giving each animal texture and intensity: the rooster's pink and purple feathers have a real fluffy softness to them and the fish is splattered with luminous colour giving it a shimmering, almost metallic, feel.

The animals are all respectfully and unsentimentally observed. The cat is a sleek and elegant predator. Her tight posture, piercing eyes and the daubs of red on her jaw and legs signal that she must be treated with caution and respect. In contrast, the dog is a lethargic and home-loving family pet. His heavily-lidded eyes and the strong lines of pink, white and yellow around his face add character and indicate that he simply wants to be curled up by a roaring fire.

Brian Wildsmith does more than introduce young children to the alphabet in this deceptively simple book: he introduces them to a celebration of his free-spirited art, where every illustration from A to Z is a vibrant and enticing painting in its own right.

Brian Wildsmith
ABC
Oxford University Press, 1962

1963

John Burningham
Borka: the Adventures of a Goose with no Feathers

John Burningham's first picture book, about a goose born with no feathers who is mocked for being different and who undertakes an adventurous journey to a place of acceptance, follows a fairytale pattern.

Borka's journey, from the sweeping marshes of the east coast of England to the security of Kew Gardens, is set against a background of stunning landscapes depicted in deep, vibrant colours. The artist combines a painterly style with the ability to convey cosy domesticity, as shown in the early illustrations of the Plumpsters and their new young family. Borka is drawn as a character with real feelings: she looks pink and vulnerable with no feathers; excited as she waits for her knitted jumper; and desolate as the other geese fly away and leave her.

The scenes from Borka's life are placed against dramatic landscapes which shimmer with paint and water effects. They are illuminated by round, vivid yellow suns or deep crimson sunsets which contrast with the dark, spiky bulrushes and reeds piercing the sky.

John Burningham's skilled use of different media gives great vitality to this book. Shape, colour and texture are used to express emotion and atmosphere: the geese who abandon Borka are drawn with thin lines and no colour and later, as they fly away, as angular abstract shapes. Thick black outlines and bright colour give Borka's refuge boat a lively, happy feel and the curved shapes and lines make the cabin appear friendly and secure. The forward movement of the boat is reflected in the outline shapes of people, animals and birds, giving these scenes an optimistic feel which is confirmed by Borka's welcome at Kew.

In this picture book John Burningham successfully combines bold lines, deep colours, painterly effects and sensitive characterisation to tell a satisfying story in a witty and moving way.

John Burningham

Borka: the Adventures of a Goose with no Feathers

Jonathan Cape, 1963

1964

C Walter Hodges
Shakespeare's Theatre

C Walter Hodges enjoys a unique reputation as an author and illustrator of vivid historical novels and as a respected scholar of the Elizabethan theatre. He combines these talents in *Shakespeare's Theatre*, a detailed illustrated history of the English theatre showing its gradual development from pagan festivals and religious dramas to the playhouses of the sixteenth century.

A particular strength of the book is the synergy that C Walter Hodges creates between text and illustration on each page. He uses a confident and free-flowing black ink line to bring vitality, movement and a sense of theatricality to each scene.

On some pages, the artist fills these inky lines with blocks of bright colour to convey the exuberance of the theatre and bring to life the troupes of clowns, jugglers, puppets, tight-rope walkers and other players. The scenes are well-grouped, full of warmth and demonstrate the artist's keen eye for composition.

A more muted colour palette is employed for those illustrations that depict the historic characters, buildings and events of Shakespeare's England. There is a meticulous draughtsman-like quality to these illustrations, as well as a strong sense of design and clever use of perspective. Close attention has also been paid to the costumes, architecture and other period details based on the artist's careful and accurate research.

This is an enjoyable information book with beautifully controlled and scholarly illustrations which reflect the artist's interest in and passion for the Elizabethan age and stage.

C Walter Hodges

Shakespeare's Theatre

Oxford University Press, 1964

1965

**Victor Ambrus
The Three Poor Tailors**

Victor Ambrus's Hungarian roots are strongly reflected in his first picture book, a simple tale with Eastern European folkloric echoes, about three poor tailors who ride into town on a single nanny goat for a day of fun which ends in disaster.

The illustrations are boldly coloured and set groups of figures, animals and buildings with black outlines against contrasting expanses of white. The large double-page illustrations with backgrounds of mountains or buildings are more sketchily drawn but are filled out with large blocks of bright colour which enhance the folkloric nature of the story. The Eastern European setting is conveyed in many details, clothes, a thatched hut with a stork on the roof, shop signs and ornamental details on the buildings.

Each tailor is drawn distinctively and the wilful nanny goat is a character in its own right. The scenes of music and dancing are well-grouped and full of life; the chase scenes show Victor Ambrus's skill at depicting scenes of action, movement and farcical mayhem. Despite the less than happy outcome for the tailors, this is a very cheerful book and the artist seems to be enjoying himself in his first picture book. It is intriguing too to note the attention to architectural details and possibly spot links to the future Time Team artist.

Victor Ambrus
The Three Poor Tailors
Oxford University Press, 1965

so the tailors ran to the window

and jumped onto the back
of the nanny-goat.

1966

Raymond Briggs
The Mother Goose Treasury

There is a wonderful Englishness to Raymond Briggs's illustrations that captures the fun and playfulness of his chosen nursery rhymes and playground songs in *The Mother Goose Treasury*.

The book has 897 illustrations in both black and white and vibrant colour; they appear in groups on each page to depict the action and add pace to the storytelling of the nursery rhymes. Some of the illustrations are placed in puddles of colour while others are boxed in a series of linear frames, perhaps an early indication of Raymond Briggs's fascination with the comic book format. Occasionally there is a strong, single image of a giant, horse or tree which leads the reader to pause and explore the artist's work. The large images of Peter the pumpkin eater and Jack jumping over the candlestick stand out as studies in colour and composition.

A range of different artistic styles and illustrative techniques are showcased in the book. There are line drawings, pen and ink sketches, bright watercolours and paper collage. Finger painting is used to add texture to trees, clouds and the sky and reinforces the simple, child-like quality and appeal of the book. The result is a sketchbook of loose and lively pictures that are full of charm and wit. The expressive faces of the characters with their strangely round and jutting chins give thought and feeling to the cast of well-known and well-loved storybook characters.

Raymond Briggs

The Mother Goose Treasury

Hamish Hamilton, 1966

THE GIANT

Fee, fi, fo, fum,
I smell the blood of an Englishman:
Be he alive or be he dead,
I'll grind his bones to make my bread.

26

Charles Keeping
Charley, Charlotte and the Golden Canary

A stunning use of vivid colour and geometric shapes characterises this story of Charley and Charlotte; friends who are separated when Charlotte leaves to live in a high-rise block of flats after the demolition of her Paradise Street home, but who are later reunited by an escaping canary.

Charles Keeping's recurrent preoccupation with the gradual disappearance of the London landscape of his childhood is reflected in the themes of this early picture book: the loss of childhood; the importance of friendship; connection with place; and the nature of freedom. The freedom of children like Charley, playing on the streets, is contrasted with the virtual imprisonment of children like Charlotte, trapped on their tower-block balconies. This is reinforced in the symbolic images of flying and caged birds, sparrows and canaries, which appear throughout the book.

The illustrations use strong colour, over-painting, sponge texturing and wax-resist techniques to fill most of the page space. Paint is allowed to run freely onto the paper, up to, and sometimes over, the text. It gives a spontaneous, exciting feel to the pictures and expresses the mood and emotion implicit in the story. Charles Keeping's use of colour is startling and memorable: deep purples, blues and a vivid pink are used alongside the bright gold and green of the canary in its cage. Colour is used symbolically to contrast old with new buildings and to link Charlotte with the canary. Geometrical shapes are combined with strong lines to give lattice, spiral and barred effects; they lend an abstract feel to the illustrations and contrast with the curved, moving shapes of the children and the flying birds.

Viewpoint is used to great effect: Charley looks up at the soaring tower block and Charlotte looks down from her balcony prison. In a characteristic use of Charles Keeping perspective, the reader also looks down from the high-rise with its straight and constricting shapes to the bustling market street below, as superimposed birds wheel in flight and a round sun sets.

Charles Keeping skilfully uses line, shape and movement to consider such themes as the nature of happiness and freedom, but what lingers most in the mind is his dazzling use of colour.

Charles Keeping
Charley, Charlotte and the Golden Canary
Oxford University Press, 1967

Because the building was so high, and the street far away below, Charlotte's mother no longer allowed her to go out to play.

1968

Pauline Baynes
A Dictionary of Chivalry

Perhaps best known as C S Lewis's and Tolkien's chosen illustrator, Pauline Baynes's illustrations in *A Dictionary of Chivalry* are typical of her talent for precise drawing that captures the movement, mood and menace of the Middle Ages.

The dictionary has more than a thousand entries that provide a detailed picture of the Knight and the things that occupied his life and thoughts. Pauline Baynes has produced an illustration that brings to life each of these entries so that the reader can see what a misericorde looks like or begin to understand what it must have been like to fight at the Battle of Crécy.

The outside margin of almost every page in the dictionary is decorated with simple black and white line drawings that describe both everyday details and elaborate pageantry. There are intricate line drawings of swords and shields; vivid depictions of dragons, griffins and other mythical beasts; and bold scenes of battles, feasts and courtly love. Each illustration is individual and all of the characters depicted have been given fully expressive features: from the coy look on a lady's face to the fear in the eyes of a fallen horse. The illustrations have been carefully researched using contemporary sources and show a studied attention to detail and feel for the age of chivalry.

There are several full-colour illustrations too which draw on a traditional medieval palette of deep reds, yellows, browns and blues. In others, Pauline Baynes has added a playful, modern twist by introducing the colour of the 1960s – the dictionary entry for horses has wonderfully bright turquoise, lime green, orange and purple steeds galloping up the margin of the page in swirling psychedelic patterns.

Grant Uden

A Dictionary of Chivalry

Illustrated by Pauline Baynes

Longmans Young Books, 1968

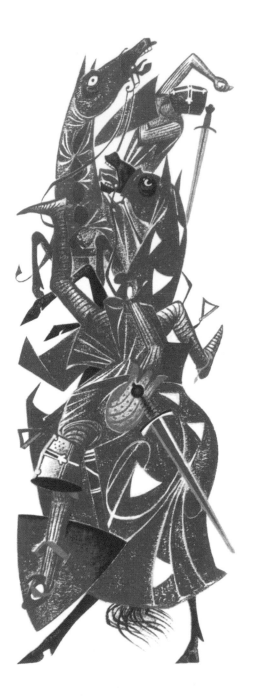

1969

Helen Oxenbury
The Quangle Wangle's Hat

In *The Quangle Wangle's Hat* Helen Oxenbury presents an exuberant interpretation of Edward Lear's famous nonsense poem with its array of eccentric, imaginary creatures.

From the endpapers filled with intertwining disc-shaped leaves to the succession of distant and close-up views of the Crumpetty Tree and its unusual occupants, Helen Oxenbury's humour and accomplished drawing techniques shine. Her use of pastel colours, detailed patterns, fine lines and intricate hatching add depth, texture and constant interest. The text is clearly set against large expanses of white background, while the contrasting shades of green leaves and grassy hills unite all the illustrations and focus attention on the quirky characters and plants.

The comic strength of this book lies in the artist's ability to interpret the creatures of the writer's imagination and to make them her own in a humorous and engaging way. The Fimble Fowl, the Pobble who has no toes, and the Dong with a luminous nose all parade across six double-page spreads looking confidently out at the reader. Each character is illustrated in great detail: the Olympian Bear's fur is drawn in a convincingly tactile way and the Dong is covered in psychedelic swirls and whorls. The Quangle Wangle's hat itself is given two large close-ups which showcase the artist's ability to depict texture; the lace and fur effects are particularly skilful.

Helen Oxenbury was awarded the 1969 Kate Greenaway Medal jointly for *The Quangle Wangle's Hat* and for her equally lively and imaginative illustrations in *The Dragon of an Ordinary Family* written by Margaret Mahy and published by Heinemann.

Edward Lear

The Quangle Wangle's Hat

Illustrated by Helen Oxenbury

Heinemann, 1969

And the small Olympian bear   And the Dong with a luminous nose

1970

John Burningham
Mr Gumpy's Outing

John Burningham's simple story of an unfortunate boat trip is a perfect balance of words and pictures. Mr Gumpy agrees to take two children and an ever-growing number of animals on a gentle punt down the river. He gives them strict instructions to behave but of course they don't and the boat capsizes.

The gentle rhythm and repetition of the story is reflected in the artist's gentle illustrative style which has a calm, timeless, almost halcyon, quality to it. On the left hand side of each double-page spread, black and white line drawings depict the journey of the boat, while on the right hand side the reader is introduced to each new animal about to board the boat.

Each page has a unique atmosphere created through a mixture of pen and ink over paint, crayon and pastel. These are not sentimental, anthropomorphic animals and there are no cartoon-like expressions on their faces; instead, their individual characters are shown in the flick of a tail or the curve of a back. Each animal is drawn distinctively and placed in a textured, colour-saturated summer landscape that's full of life and light. The artist's affinity with the natural environment is obvious throughout the book.

John Burningham's distinctive illustrative style is spare and he keeps his drawing down to the bare minimum; the result is a confident and painterly picture book about the happiness of summer days spent in the countryside.

John Burningham
Mr Gumpy's Outing
Jonathan Cape, 1970

Jan Pieńkowski
The Kingdom under the Sea

Polish artist Jan Pieńkowski left his native Warsaw during the Second World War and arrived in England aged ten. He was fittingly awarded his first Kate Greenaway Medal for his magical and distinctive illustrations in this collection of traditional Eastern European folk tales.

The Kingdom under the Sea continues the collaboration between Jan Pieńkowski and writer Joan Aiken and showcases the artist's trademark use of black silhouettes against marbled paper backgrounds, a technique inspired by the paper-cuts he had seen as a child in Poland. The black paper-cut shapes stand out sharply from the vibrant background colours which are also informed by memories of Polish folk art.

Jan Pieńkowski uses his silhouette style to dramatic effect to create the perfect atmosphere of mystery, romance and menace required by a folk tale collection of goblins, witches, knights, enchanted castles and undersea kingdoms. The black silhouettes curve and dance through the book, shaping and twining around the text, crossing the length of double-pages and, at intervals, filling a full page. The illustrations are full of movement, so that hair floats in the sea, briars creep and candle smoke drifts over the page. The delicate details of feathers and spindly twigs, achieved using only pieces of paper, are truly amazing and their tiny features can all be picked out.

Where colour is used, the effects are startling. The illuminated letters lent a manuscript-like feel. The Sun Lord's castle looks like an Art Deco stained-glass window and the orange of Baba Yaga's oven jolts the reader. Menace and humour are combined in these illustrations, as in the nose-thumbing goblins, the grinning sea monster and the drunken elephants dancing on a grapevine.

Jan Pieńkowski has succeeded in bringing an Eastern European atmosphere to his illustrations which perfectly match the written stories and make the world they describe accessible. He has created a visual style that is original and instantly recognisable.

Joan Aiken
The Kingdom under the Sea
Illustrated by Jan Pieńkowski
Jonathan Cape, 1971

1972

Krystyna Turska
The Woodcutter's Duck

This Polish story about a poor woodcutter with a kind heart and magical powers is sumptuously illustrated in the colours and style of Eastern European folk-art. The setting and tradition of the story are enhanced by the detailed village scenes of thatched houses, dancing peasants and wandering farmyard animals.

The mountain landscape is painted in delicate shades of green and brown. The triangular shapes of the fields and mountains are patterned with trees and flowers giving patchwork effects to some pages. The arrival of the Great Hetman and his soldiers into the village brings much brighter colour to the illustrations in the tunics, sashes, flags and banners. Small patches of white are visible through the colour as if the ink has been dabbed from the page, giving the impression that the pictures have been painted onto wood and are worn with age. This effect is augmented by the soft broken lines bordering each double-page spread.

When the Great Hetman attempts to eat the duck, the woodcutter lets loose a magical storm. The energy of the wind and rain howls across the page in swirling lines, capturing the soldiers and tossing them about in patterns of jumbled colour. The soldiers are drawn alike and their collective misery is humorously depicted in their sloped shoulders and drooping moustaches. Their unhappiness is short-lived, though, as the woodcutter and his duck are chosen to lead the army in the Great Hetman's place. The final image of the village, now decorated with golden trees and sunflowers, brings the reader full circle and gives the book its totally satisfying ending.

Krystyna Turska

The Woodcutter's Duck

Hamish Hamilton, 1972

Immediately the sky grew black. Rain came pouring down with such force that in a few seconds the ground was flooded. The water rose and rose until the whole army, the Great Hetman included, were up to their necks in it.

Bartek, with his duck at his feet,

looked down at the ridiculous sight. "Do you still want to eat my friend?" he asked.

"I shall never touch her—I won't let anyone lay a finger on a feather of hers," said the Great Hetman. "I promise. Just stop this rain!"

1973

Raymond Briggs
Father Christmas

Raymond Briggs brings his expertise with the comic-strip form to the story of a cantankerous Father Christmas who rather reluctantly harnesses his reindeer, climbs down chimneys and delivers presents to sleeping children on Christmas Eve.

Raymond Briggs builds on the traditional depiction of Father Christmas as a cuddly, white-haired, rosy-cheeked old man, giving him an unexpected grumpiness and hatred for the winter season. His changing emotions are shown in the detail of his dotted eyes and dashed eyebrows, as well as through the speech bubbles by which Father Christmas speaks directly from the page. Other illustrative details give Father Christmas an endearing back-story: he lives in a comfortable home with an outside lavatory, longs for lazy days sunbathing at the beach and likes a drink or two. The illustrations are precisely drawn and coloured pastel crayons are used to give them a lovely softness. Perspective is well used throughout the book: houses are viewed from the sky, from the street, and through cross-sections, encouraging the reader to be nosy and explore.

The strength of his book, though, is in the totality of its design and Raymond Briggs's sophisticated control over his artwork. The comic-book format allows the artist room to include much more than is possible in a traditional picture book. The varying number of frames placed on each page add pace and rhythm to the storytelling. Lots of frames in quick succession are used to build tension. A clock appears in several of these frames to covey urgency as Father Christmas struggles with television aerials, stairs, and a seemingly impenetrable caravan. Smaller frames open out into large single or double-page spreads where the reader is encouraged to pause, explore the detail, and help Father Christmas find his way along streets and into the waiting houses.

Raymond Briggs
Father Christmas
Hamish Hamilton, 1973

1974

Pat Hutchins
The Wind Blew

Pat Hutchins tells a simple rhyming story about a windy day with text and illustrations combining perfectly as, one by one, the characters' belongings are swept up into the air and a chaotic and comic chase to retrieve them ensues.

The title page is effective in its use of shape and pattern to depict the effect of the wind on the trees as trunks bow and branches bend. Contrasting green tones are subtly used and small paint lines give the impression of moving leaves and sleeting rain as Mr White, the first character to be buffeted by the wind, struggles with his umbrella.

The wind blew.

The chase for lost belongings moves from the countryside to the town, leading the reader on from page to page at a fast pace. The pattern of bricks on buildings replace the earlier leaf patterns and the background colour changes from green to brown and grey. The cumulative style of the text and illustrations is enhanced by a build up of colour and detail; the focus of the illustration also shifts upwards to the jumble of lost belongings set against a plain white background.

Readers are able to bring their predicting, counting and sorting skills to bear as items are snatched up, muddled and dropped before the wind finally blows away to sea.

In **The Wind Blew** Pat Hutchins demonstrates her trademark skill of combining a clear text with strongly sequenced illustrations to create a simple and satisfying narrative full of bright colours, detail, movement and humour.

Pat Hutchins

The Wind Blew

The Bodley Head, 1974

1975

Victor Ambrus
Mishka

Like Victor Ambrus's previous picture books, there is a strong Eastern European feel to this folktale about a young boy called Mishka who runs away to the circus to seek fame and fortune with his fiddle.

Eleven double-page spreads are filled with brightly coloured illustrations of different circus scenes set against stark white backgrounds. The design and composition of each page effectively conveys the excitement and drama of the circus, as Mishka flies on the trapeze, plays with the clowns and balances on the head of an elephant. The distinctive illustrations are drawn in bold inky lines and are filled with strong colours, particularly yellows and reds, which add punch to the page. Many details suggest the story's Eastern European roots and setting, including the wooden buildings, the circus caravans and the clothes worn by the people in the crowds.

The circus performers are all drawn distinctively and are given their own individual characters. The ringmaster is a pantomime villain with a pointed nose, black cape and top hat; and the trapeze artists are burly, muscled and tattooed bullies. The animals are equally expressive. The total disdain of the elephants is shown in their huge backsides and with just a flick of their tails; and the frightening unpredictability of the caged lions comes across in tight body postures and powerful eyes. This is a playful picture book with a cast of wonderful characters and a completely satisfying ending.

Victor Ambrus was awarded the 1975 Kate Greenaway Medal jointly for **Mishka** and for **Horses in Battle**, an illustrated history of the use of horses in warfare also published by Oxford University Press.

Victor Ambrus

Mishka

Oxford University Press, 1975

1976

Gail E Haley
The Post Office Cat

Gail E Haley has the distinction of being the only illustrator to have won the Kate Greenaway Medal and its American equivalent, the Caldecott Medal. Her characteristic use of artistic techniques that reflect the period and culture of her books' settings is evident in this story of Clarence, a cat who escapes the comfort of the farmyard in search of a better life on the streets of Victorian London. Clarence eventually finds fame and fortune as the Post Office cat with no shortage of mice to keep him busy and replete.

The story, based on historical fact, is enhanced by the artist's illustrations created using Victorian lithographic techniques. The use of a landscape format for the book means that each double-page spread offers the reader panoramic views of London's streets, parks, shops and docks. The affluence and poverty of the Victorian age are both depicted. Each double-page illustration is beautifully framed combining a thick black line with an object integral to the picture: the arm of a ship's sail; the wheel of a carriage; an ironwork gas lamp. The frames work by positioning the reader as an active and empathetic observer of the action.

The illustrations are drawn with bold black and grey lines and, while simply outlined, contain a wealth of historic detail. Some illustrations are left unfilled while others are completed with solid blocks of colour. Colour is used to reflect the changing seasons, mood and atmosphere as the story progresses. Bright colours reflect the warmth and hopefulness of the park in the summer, while more muted tones are used to depict the cold, hunger and fear of the Dickensian winter streets. The artist's greatest strength in her illustrations, however, is that by using traditional techniques, she has created a picture book that brings Victorian London to life for young readers.

Gail E Haley

The Post Office Cat

The Bodley Head, 1976

1977

Shirley Hughes
Dogger

It is not surprising that *Dogger* was voted the public's favourite Kate Greenaway Medal winner in the award's fiftieth anniversary year, as the story of a much-loved toy which is lost and then found again, is one with which children and families can always identify. The warmth, humour and quality of loving observation which Shirley Hughes brings to bear on this domestic drama have made her early picture book an established classic.

Dogger looks out from the page in the first large illustration. He is a believably real toy; his creased paws, worn thread nose and stitched ears make the reader want to pick him up and hold him almost as much as Dave does. The original Dogger did belong to one of Shirley Hughes's children and the idea of the story began when he fell out of a cupboard one day, prompting memories of earlier lost toy dramas in the family. The cover illustration and an early sequence of small action illustrations show the reader, through a convincing portrayal of body language and expression, how much Dave loves Dogger. Shirley Hughes puts the child's experience at the centre of the book and young children can follow Dave's increasingly distressed expressions and identify with the narrative completely.

Sketchbook studies of children are the source of the artist's fictional characters. Her flowing line and colour washes capture the positions and movements of children very accurately: Dave's flowing hair stands on end as he sleeps; Bella is always moving; and baby Joe reaches out, trying to join in. The illustrations are full of humour and witty observations of the everyday routines, chaos and clutter of family life. Composition and viewpoint are used effectively to tell the story as full-page illustrations, cartoon-style action sequences, split-screens, an aerial view and close-ups combine to move the narrative along and give the reader plenty of details and visual clues.

Shirley Hughes has said that a picture book is a drama; her skill here is to combine artistic techniques with empathy to portray the everyday life of a loving family. She brings drama to a recognisable situation to create a heart-warming picture book which has been a firm favourite for thirty years.

Shirley Hughes
Dogger
The Bodley Head, 1977

Once there was a soft brown toy called Dogger. One of his ears pointed upwards and the other flopped over. His fur was worn in places because he was quite old. He belonged to Dave.

1978

Janet Ahlberg
Each Peach Pear Plum

Each Peach Pear Plum is a deceptively simple, engaging picture book in which Janet Ahlberg's gentle pen and watercolour illustrations complement her husband Allan's text to give young children the pleasure and satisfaction of using their knowledge of nursery rhymes to interact with the book, spot clues and find hidden characters.

The use of twining branches, flowers, curved leaves, rounded fruit and appealing animals gives the book a William Morris-like style with complete child appeal. The book is very carefully designed to lead the reader through a range of settings filled with recognisable images from the literature of childhood. The reader is led from the opening, quilt-like view of fields, cottage and an orchard of peach, pear and plum trees, into Mother Hubbard's kitchen, up Jack and Jill's hill, and out into Robin Hood's forest. Each double-page spread follows a simple picture frame format with text and a small pictorial clue on one side, balanced by a detailed full-frame illustration with objects to find on the other.

Janet Ahlberg's fondness for collecting artefacts is obvious in her loving depictions of old-fashioned mangles, copper kettles, broomsticks and churns which match the nursery rhyme theme. Throughout the book, the reader is encouraged to make links and connections by following the running story of Baby Bunting and his misadventures and by spotting clever details, such as the reassuring tin of dog food in Mother Hubbard's kitchen cupboard.

There is something very pleasing in seeing the domestic lives of familiar characters represented in such a witty way. The artist's ability to depict a happily comfortable world, shown to great effect in the final full-page illustration where she completes the circular story and reunites all the characters, makes this a very enjoyable and satisfying book.

Allan Ahlberg

Each Peach Pear Plum

Illustrated by Janet Ahlberg

Viking Kestrel, 1978

1979

Jan Pieńkowski
Haunted House

Jan Pieńkowski led a renaissance in the pop-up genre with the publication of *Haunted House* in 1979. The now-famous green front door, with its beckoning note to "let yourself in" tucked above the door handle, encourages the reader to enter the spooky house. Once inside, and with only a single line of text on each page, Pieńkowski encourages the reader to search each room of the house, opening doors and drawers or lifting toilet seats, to discover the dark secrets hidden there. It's a multi-layered book. The reader travels from room to room in the company of two mice unknowingly pursued by a hungry black cat. Through the window in each room there is also the glimpse of an alien space-ship; it gets closer on each page and finally bursts through the bathroom wall.

The illustrations have a bold, cartoon-like quality and are brightly coloured with strong use of texture and pattern on the wood, wallpaper and fabrics. The strength of this book, however, is in its clever and masterfully produced paper engineering which encourages anticipation and interaction. Each double-page spread acts like a stage set: monsters, aliens and skeletons leap out at the reader; a crocodile lurches out of the bath; a ghost slowly appears above the four-poster bed; and a bat spreads its wings ominously beyond the limits of the page. This is a book that demands and rewards exploration from every possible angle because the illustrations are packed full of interesting and witty details: from Dracula's wedding photograph to Long John Silver's treasure chest hidden in the attic.

Jan Pieńkowski
Haunted House
Heinemann, 1979

1980 Quentin Blake
Mister Magnolia

Mister Magnolia is the archetypal English eccentric dressed in a shabby frock coat, enormous bow tie, clashing colours and only one boot. This simple and charmingly dotty story, told in rhyme, reveals more about Mister Magnolia's flamboyant lifestyle and follows him in his search for that elusive second shoe.

The liveliness of the rhyme is enhanced by the energetic, exuberant and humorous illustrations. Mister Magnolia and the cast of supporting characters are each drawn with confident economy; they are given their own quirky personalities through well-observed arm movements, a flick of hair, a wayward scarf or a wonky ear. There is no hesitation in Quentin Blake's penmanship and he uses broad sweeps of colour to create an immediacy and freshness on every page.

The composition of each double-page spread encourages and rewards detailed looking. Small, seemingly insignificant details paint a picture of Mister Magnolia as a kindly, well-loved gentleman with a fondness for tea and biscuits who has fallen on hard times and is reduced to using wooden packing cases as tables and chairs.

The book has a real sense of movement too. Mister Magnolia performs a series of ballet-like poses throughout the book complete with outstretched toes and fingers. Even his nose acts as a pointer to the frenzied action that surrounds or follows him. Sketchily drawn mice, owls, toads, parakeets and other animals dance across the pages, adding to the sense of movement and reinforcing the fast pace and strong rhythm of the story.

Quentin Blake is the master of simple line and wash illustrations. This book is full of joy: wild lines and vibrant colours leap from every page, making the whole work fresh, unique and memorable.

Quentin Blake
Mister Magnolia
Jonathan Cape, 1980

1981

Charles Keeping
The Highwayman

Charles Keeping's second Kate Greenaway Medal-winning book saw him move from the vivid colour blocks of his earlier picture books for younger children to produce the first in a series of powerfully intense, picture books for older readers in monochrome. These line and tone illustrations, printed in dark brown and black, are perfectly suited to the mood of Alfred Noyes's narrative poem about the doomed love between the Highwayman and Bess, the landlord's daughter.

The poem itself is full of colourful description and the lack of colour in the illustrations increases the dramatic tension and frees the reader's imagination. The illustrations completely surround the text, bleeding to the edges of the page, powerfully confirming Charles Keeping's belief that the writer and artist share the task of filling the paper and telling the story. A sense of movement is brilliantly conveyed by the use of line, as in the endpapers where the streaming hairs of mane and tail reflect the horse's galloping motion. The violence and aggression implicit in the text are made explicit in the illustrations: the soldiers cruelly manhandle Bess; the maddened Highwayman sits astride his horse seemingly about to burst from the page; and, finally, his dead body lays sprawling and bleeding on the ground. These disturbing and powerfully composed images have a shocking impact but add to the understanding of the poem.

Charles Keeping's adept and considered use of viewpoint, perspective and design are strongly evident throughout the book. The reader constantly looks in through a textured frame to observe characters, or looks out to watch the sparse landscape of winding roads and gaunt trees with a feeling of ominous expectation. This characteristic window-frame viewpoint links back to the artist's childhood spent drawing from his London window vantage point. The use of a consistent horizon line creates unity; and the fact that the final five pages and back endpapers are black-to-white reversals of the opening sequence of drawings counterpoints perfectly the ghostly effect of the poem's ending.

The combination of Charles Keeping's complete mastery of artistic techniques and his ability to capture mood and emotion ensure that a reading of **The Highwayman** becomes a powerful, if sometimes overwhelming, experience.

Alfred Noyes

The Highwayman

Illustrated by Charles Keeping

Oxford University Press, 1981

1982

Michael Foreman
Sleeping Beauty and Other Favourite Fairy Tales

In his first Kate Greenaway Medal-winning book, Michael Foreman delivers a fresh interpretation of twelve magical fairytales complete with ogres, witches and dream-like castles. A limited number of line drawings and watercolour paintings are used to illustrate each fairytale, each one capturing the essence and emotion of the story. The brutal details of the original Charles Perrault stories are still there but, in Michael Foreman's hands, they are balanced with tenderness and occasional humour. In *Cinderella*, for instance, blood pours from one sister's toes while two servants support the other sister as she crams her foot into the slipper in an almost slapstick scene.

The use of colour is dramatic. There are strong hues of turquoise in the night skies and delicate washes of pink and orange in some landscape scenes. The artist sees and reads colour to great effect, so that there are blended shades of pink, yellow, ochre and mauve in the flesh tones of his kings, princesses and giants. The pencil drawings and line and wash illustrations evoke a range of moods and atmosphere, from the ghostly haunting of the trackless forest to the candlelit intimacy of the Beast's castle. The sheer size and scale of the forest is skillfully drawn as are the sweeping landscapes of fields and mountains. There is lots of clever visual detailing in each picture, as in *Little Red Riding Hood* where the wolf's teeth are in a glass by the bed or in *Bluebeard* where the skull-shaped castle predicts the horrible reality that lies hidden inside.

Michael Foreman was awarded the 1982 Kate Greenaway Medal jointly for *Sleeping Beauty and Other Favourite Fairy Tales* and for the illustrations to his dinosaur story, *Long Neck and Thunderfoot*, published by Viking Kestrel.

Angela Carter

Sleeping Beauty and Other Favourite Fairy Tales

Illustrated by Michael Foreman

Victor Gollancz, 1982

1983

Anthony Browne
Gorilla

Anthony Browne won the Kurt Maschler Award as well as the Kate Greenaway Medal for *Gorilla*, a powerful story of emotional isolation and loneliness with illustrations demonstrating the artist's characteristic use of symbolism, surrealism and witty visual jokes.

Anthony Browne uses gorillas to throw light on human behaviour and is fascinated by the contrasting strength and gentleness they represent. This fascination with gorillas is mirrored by Hannah, the central character, who focuses on gorillas as a way of dealing with the emotional distance and coldness of her father. The disappointing toy gorilla she receives as a birthday present turns into a fantasy gorilla who acts as a stand-in father in an extended dream sequence full of surrealistic details and film references. The influence of film on the artist's style appears in pictures of the gorilla as King Kong and Superman, in the Fred and Ginger dancing gorillas and in the sequencing of images throughout the book.

Anthony Browne uses colour, light and shade and strong black frames to reflect a bleak mood of loneliness and disconnection. Hannah's father is pale, blocked in by lines and box shapes; there are constant barriers between him and his daughter. Shadows, lines and bars throughout the illustrations represent real prisons, like the zoo, and self-imposed, emotional ones. The only bright colour is the red that Hannah wears and she always appears in a pool of light threatened by the surrounding dark shadows and oppressive patterns. The colour red appears as a symbol of hope and life and the final illustration, when Hannah's father wears red too, promises a happier future with connection replacing isolation.

This is a sophisticated, emotionally-affecting picture book with thoughtful illustrations which reflect the artist's influences and concerns while telling a moving story.

Anthony Browne

Gorilla

Julia MacRae Books, 1983

1984

Errol Le Cain
Hiawatha's Childhood

The hypnotic rhythm and rich language of Longfellow's poem *The Song of Hiawatha* is matched by Errol Le Cain's intense illustrations, in which he details the legends and wisdom of Hiawatha's people and the splendour of the natural world around him.

Errol Le Cain draws attention to the beauty of the poet's words by setting them against contrasting backgrounds; the result encourages the reader to look at the words first and then explore the pictures. A border is given to each double-page spread incorporating rich Native American patterns which are also reflected in the Grandmother's shawl and the baby's swaddling. Simple motifs of flowers, leaves and birds are used to emphasise Hiawatha's cultural heritage and the Native Americans' unity with their environment.

Colour is used effectively throughout the book to convey the different seasons and help the reader empathise with the natural rhythms of the world in which Hiawatha is growing up. There is a warm yellow and orange sheen over the lake in the autumn and a cold grey-green winter scene with white frosted patterns above the trees. A fiery sun and a bright rainbow are spread across other pages.

The composition of the pages, with Hiawatha cuddled up with his Grandmother or enclosed by trees, give the book a feeling of complete safety. All the illustrations have a softness and stillness to them. The artist's background in animated films is clearly visible, not only in the attention to detail but also in the quiet movement of the illustrations, so that the smoke from Grandmother's pipe gently curls around the sides of her wigwam and a lone kayak glides peacefully across the lake.

Henry Wadsworth Longfellow

Hiawatha's Childhood

Illustrated by Errol Le Cain

Faber and Faber, 1984

1985

Juan Wijngaard
Sir Gawain and the Loathly Lady

This is a retelling of the medieval romance tale about a beautiful woman who is transformed into an ugly hag until released from the enchantment by her husband who allows her to choose her own future. It is a story that recurs throughout literature: in Celtic myth, ballads and in Chaucerian and Arthurian tales. The illustrations in this version subtly reflect these multiple origins.

Juan Wijngaard shows a miniaturist's skill throughout this book. His meticulously detailed paintings are full of the colours, opulent fabrics and symbols of medieval pageantry. They effectively set the story in a time of courtliness and chivalry which the reader observes from outside the frames. Borders and patterns frame the text and illustrations with the fitting precision of an illuminated manuscript.

The illustrations are brilliantly naturalistic with wintry forest and lakeside backgrounds full of closely observed details from the natural world, including dead bracken, fallen leaves and early morning mists. The interior views are more stylised; they complement the colours and symbolism of the borders and show the artist's great skill at painting rich fabrics and revealing facial expressions. The recurring appearance of squares and chess board motifs reinforces the themes of riddle-solving and chivalrous game-playing.

The use of stylised effects, symbolism and realistic settings is continued in the artist's portrayal of character. Arthur's expression shows concern; Guinevere's kindness breaks through the courtly restraints; and the depiction of the Loathly Lady is both shocking and poignant as she stares directly out of the page at the reader.

Selina Hastings
Sir Gawain and the Loathly Lady
Illustrated by Juan Wijngaard
Walker Books, 1985

'My honour is at stake,' he said. 'I do not know how I may save it.'

Sir Gawain, the youngest of the company, was sitting close by playing chess. On hearing Arthur's words he leapt up, scattering the ivory chessmen at his feet. 'Sire, I beg you, let *me* defend you! Grant *me* the quest, that I may be the one to save the honour of my King!'

1986

Fiona French
Snow White in New York

Fiona French's characteristic love of colour and flat pattern are evident in this witty re-telling of **Snow White** which transposes the traditional tale to 1930s America, and has the wicked stepmother as Queen of the New York Underworld, the seven dwarves as jazz musicians and the prince as a moody, chisel-jawed newspaper reporter. The mirror in which the stepmother likes to look at herself, and which later reports Snow White's beauty, is no ordinary wall-mounted looking-glass, but a salacious newspaper called The New York Mirror. It is a wonderfully witty touch, clearly demonstrating the multi-layered nature of this picture book.

The story is told in clear, direct and spare language, leaving the illustrations to add the all-important detail in a series of fourteen double-page spreads. All the illustrations have enormous visual impact; they are bled to the very edges of the page with no frames to contain them, so that the reader has the feeling of being pulled into and almost surrounded by the pictures.

The illustrations are all beautifully designed in an elegant Art Deco style which vividly reinforce the period and setting of the story. Strong vertical lines, chevron patterns, zigzags, jumbled shapes and sunburst motifs fill each page, with other Art Deco details picked out in the background architecture and costumes. The use of sharp lines of colour to create a shimmering effect, combined with distinctive geometric shapes, are reminiscent of the work of the op-artist, Bridget Riley, for whom Fiona French worked as an assistant in the 1960s.

Colour dominates this book. There are great shafts of orange and yellow light; atmospheric tones of blue that add a sense of intimacy to the nightclub scenes; explosions of red and pink to bring drama; and simple black silhouettes.

Fiona French

Snow White in New York

Oxford University Press, 1986

1987

Adrienne Kennaway
Crafty Chameleon

Adrienne Kennaway grew up in Kenya and her background, together with a love of the natural world, informs her illustrations to this traditional African folk tale. The simple moral story of a clever chameleon, who outwits the bullying leopard and crocodile, is illustrated with vivid watercolour pictures which brilliantly depict the African landscape, vegetation and wildlife.

From the front cover, with its vibrant greens and yellows and overlapping leaf shapes, into the main story, with its succession of brightly detailed double-page spreads, Adrienne Kennaway uses colour, pattern, shape and perspective to bring the story to life. The page space is filled with spreading foliage, plains patterned with stones and spiky shrubs, and atmospheric river scenes. The clever positioning of the animals always draws the readers' eye. Mouth lines, eye and body shapes convey mood and expression; the long crocodile and rounded leopard outlines contrast particularly effectively.

The artist is skilled at painting action sequences: chameleon falls from a tree; crocodile lunges out of the river; animals pull in the tug-of-war scenes. The viewpoint changes throughout the story as the eye is drawn from ground to treetop to river bed. The shades, tones and shapes achieved by overlapping watercolour paints and the use of traditional batik effects add to the atmosphere.

The final double-page spread is a reminder of the cover illustration. Dazzling yellows and oranges and a shining sun reflect the chameleon's success and bring a happy ending to this tale which is greatly enhanced by Adrienne Kennaway's feel for the landscape, wildlife and traditions of Africa.

Mwenye Hadithi

Crafty Chameleon

Illustrated by Adrienne Kennaway

Hodder and Stoughton, 1987

Then Crocodile pulled hard, and Leopard was dragged through a nest of biting ants.

1988

Barbara Firth
Can't You Sleep, Little Bear?

Big Bear and Little Bear make their first appearance in this gentle and comforting bedtime story which marks the beginning of a fruitful relationship between Martin Waddell's words and Barbara Firth's subtle illustrations. The problem of a sleepless night in the bear cave are solved by the love and patience of Big Bear, as he tries to show Little Bear that he need not be afraid of the dark. When a succession of lanterns does not help, Big Bear offers the moon, a sky full of twinkling stars and his own comforting arms to help send Little Bear to sleep.

Barbara Firth's admitted bias towards illustrating natural history, and the hours spent carefully watching and recording the movements and habits of bears in a zoo, make her the perfect illustrator for this story. The calm landscapes and beautifully drawn bears remain convincing, while also showing the characteristics of a loving parent and wilful child.

The interior illustrations are contained in framed arch shapes with muted watercolour backgrounds, rounded shapes and softly drawn outlines. Balance is achieved by placing illustrated, text-filled frames opposite each other. The frames are surrounded by a shaded blue and grey background, reflecting the contrast between the cosy world of the cave and the surrounding darkness.

Barbara Firth fills the cave scenes with amusing and homely details which enhance the warm atmosphere, for instance, Big Bear's wonderfully squashy chair has claws and bear feet and the shape and position of Little Bear's toy increasingly reflects his sleeplessness. The outdoor scenes use the whole page and so break the sequence of frames to add impact. The illustration of the two bears climbing the stairs hand in hand is strikingly composed, as the reader's eye follows them to the cave entrance. The final double-page spread uses shape, colour, tone and light effects to convey an atmosphere of complete comfort and reassurance, thereby creating an ideal ending to this calming bedtime book.

Martin Waddell

Can't You Sleep, Little Bear?

Illustrated by Barbara Firth

Walker Books, 1988

And Big Bear read the Bear Book right to ...

1989

Michael Foreman
War Boy: a Country Childhood

Historical detail is packed into every page of Michael Foreman's memoir of growing up in wartime Suffolk. The book opens dramatically with a fire-bomb coming through the roof of the room where young Michael is sleeping; a double-page spread illustrates his family's escape from the burning house in washes of flaming pink, crimson and yellow. His early memories are recorded with simplicity and humour, illustrating the arrival of the Americans, the embarrassment of using the outside lavatory and his first encounters with films and bananas. The images showing children exploring beaches and bomb-sites and playing Cowboys and Indians express the freedom and adventure of his boyhood. As well as these narrative pictures, the artist also loads his illustrations with technical details and annotated plans of barrage balloons and doodlebugs. The inclusion of photographs and other artefacts add authenticity to the text.

A range of different artistic styles are used in the book. Pen and ink sketches are combined with line and wash landscapes of vast skies and open spaces. There are also bright domestic scenes of soldiers and sailors drinking tea in the village shop and playing cards around the dinner table. These images are often brought into sharp focus by the accompanying text which documents the harsh realities of the war. Colour is beautifully used throughout the book. Michael Foreman covers the paper with loose and luminous washes of watercolour to create settings and scenes. His trademark use of turquoise blue is evident, but greens, reds and pinks are used to equally great effect. The final images of the harvest in shades of golden yellow are visually stunning.

Michael Foreman's understanding of the picture book format for young children and his dextrous skill as an artist are used well in this book to create an accessible and richly detailed story of his wartime childhood.

Michael Foreman
War Boy: a Country Childhood
Pavilion Books, 1989

One result of the bombing was that millions of seeds would be blown out of gardens and showered around the district. The following spring and summer, piles of rubble burst into bloom. Marigolds, irises and, best of all, potatoes sprouted everywhere.

1990

Gary Blythe
The Whales' Song

Gary Blythe's first picture book tells the story of Lilly, a young girl so entranced by her grandmother's tales of an ocean once filled with whales, that she longs to hear their song for herself.

The poetic and dream-like story is enhanced by Gary Blythe's breathtakingly beautiful oil paintings. The artist started painting in oils when he was fifteen years old and his mastery of the medium is clearly demonstrated throughout the book. His illustrations mix atmospheric seascapes with movingly realistic portraits that reflect the haunting theme of the story. Page space is used well. Blocks of text are carefully placed in framed panels against white backgrounds, leaving room for the reader to explore every inch of the large paintings.

The illustrations contrast light and shade to great effect. Light shines through the sea to illuminate the curved shapes of the whales; the faces of Lilly and her grandmother are lit to highlight their contrasting skin tones and hair texture; sand and sunsets glows in bright and richly painted colours; and moonlight shines on Lilly's face as she looks out of her window or watches the whales leap from the sea.

Composition and perspective are skilfully used as the reader's viewpoint of the cottage interior changes to reflect mood; faces are shown in close-up to convey character; and, as she dreams, Lilly's bedroom merges into a strikingly composed sea-scene full of curved whale shapes. Attention to detail can be seen in the realistic clutter inside the cottage and in touches like the delicate sea spray or the tiny flower floating on the dark sea.

This is a story about the power of the imagination and the importance of dreams. Gary Blythe's atmospheric illustrations match these themes perfectly and make this book one that lingers long in the mind's eye.

Dyan Sheldon

The Whales' Song

Illustrated by Gary Blythe

Hutchinson, 1990

1991

Janet Ahlberg
The Jolly Christmas Postman

Janet Ahlberg won her second Kate Greenaway Medal for the second in a series of three books about the Jolly Postman, the product of years of painstaking work by Janet and her husband Allan Ahlberg and inspired by their daughter's childhood fascination with letters and envelopes.

The reader follows the Jolly Postman through a series of subtly coloured and playfully detailed pen and watercolour illustrations as he cycles across a snowy landscape on Christmas Eve, delivering cards and letters to familiar characters. Envelopes containing cards, games, a jigsaw, a tiny book and an intricate peep show are interspersed at intervals throughout the pages. The ingenious use of paper engineering techniques, combined with witty illustrations and text, make this a perfectly designed and produced book.

Each item of humorously personalised post can be read as the characters themselves are reading them. Close reading and looking is repaid with many happy discoveries, jokes and connections: Baby Bear and Goldilocks have new siblings; Humpty Dumpty is given a nine-piece jigsaw by the King's men and horses; the registration number for the Three Little Pigs' van is 01 NKS; and Cat and Fiddle references recur throughout the book.

Janet Ahlberg's work displays a miniaturist's skill: for instance, the illustration of the Gingerbread Boy opening his book within a book in the doorway of his biscuit tin house, while the Jolly Postman drinks a bucketful of tea and nibbles twenty four tiny mice pies. This book also demonstrates a mastery of inter-textual references to storybook characters and to previous Ahlberg works: Baby Bunting appears in Red Riding Hood's game and the Gingerbread Boy's Christmas annual contains a rhyme called 'Peaches and Plums'. This level of attention to detail, combined with the witty and endearing portrayal of the family life of familiar characters, results in a pleasurable reading experience which bears frequent repetition.

Allan Ahlberg

The Jolly Christmas Postman

Illustrated by Janet Ahlberg

Heinemann, 1991

'A book in a book!' says the Gingerbread Boy.
  'What a simply *delicious* surprise.'
(But if only he knew, *he's* in one, too –
  That really would open his eyes.)
Then …
  A bucket of tea for the Postman
And four and twenty mince pies.

1992

Anthony Browne
Zoo

Anthony Browne won his second Kate Greenaway Medal for **Zoo**, a witty and moving story of one family's trip to the zoo to look at the animals in their cages. It is packed full of the artist's characteristic use of symbolism, surrealist detail and witty visual puns, as well as providing a serious message to its young readers.

Throughout the book, Anthony Browne uses contrasting visual styles to represent the family and the animals. Cartoon-like images, bright colours and comic book techniques, such as speech bubbles, are used to depict the family. Each image is lightly framed and often the characters or speech bubbles burst out emphasizing the freedom of the world outside the cages. In contrast, the animals are given a more realistic, almost photographic, artistic treatment. Perspective, pattern, shadow and heavy black frames are used to reinforce the isolation, loneliness and disconnection of the animals who are predominately positioned alone, behind fences and against brick walls, with their bodies or faces turned away from the reader.

The position in which the artist places the reader is important. The reader, like the family, is always the distanced observer of the various animals; however, a subtle shift takes place as the book progresses and increasingly the family is seen from the animal's viewpoint. They are now the ones behind the walls and fences, beautifully shown in the final image of the boy alone and seemingly caged in his room.

Anthony Browne's characteristic surrealist detail and visual jokes are used to play with the reader's understanding of what is animal and what is human. Men and women are shown wearing leather jackets, fur coats and leopard-skin trousers; there is a man with a pig's head and a woman with reptilian feet. There are visual references to other artists, such as Magritte, Dali, Van Gogh, Edward Hopper and David Hockney, as well as nods to cultural icons, including Cat Woman who makes an appearance in a crowd scene.

This book gives children the space to think as well as be entertained. It's a teasing and visually stunning examination of the relationship between humans and animals and the role of zoos.

Anthony Browne

Zoo

Julia MacRae Books, 1992

1993

Alan Lee
Black Ships Before Troy

Alan Lee's skill as an exciting illustrator of fantasy books and his love of mythology are revealed in his haunting and dramatic images for this re-telling of the Iliad.

Patterned borders and narrow band-shaped illustrations are used as chapter headings to reflect the classical origins of the story. As the text widens to cover the detail and depth of the Trojan War, the illustrations expand to frame and surround the text and to fill large parts of the double-page spreads.

The misty watercolour illustrations depicting seas, ships, hillsides, gods and goddesses are painted in a subdued range of brown, blue and silver grey shades. The haunting, ethereal feel achieved by this colour palette is increased by the lack of black outlines. The pale, dreamy style is combined with great attention to detail, particularly in the folds and shapes of armour, the weapons, ships, horses and battles. Where colour is used, as in the bold red of a helmet or a blood-filled river, the effect is dramatic.

By contrasting atmospheric images from the romantic traditions of illustration with harsh and chaotic action scenes, Alan Lee ensures his images are perfectly in keeping with the tensions and demands of a mythic tale about a brutal war. The style perhaps prefigures his future role as a conceptual artist for Peter Jackson's *Lord of the Rings* trilogy and a move from the Kate Greenaway Medal for illustration to an Academy Award for Best Art Direction.

Alan Lee

Black Ships Before Troy

Frances Lincoln, 1993

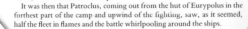

Men tore brands from the trampled cooking fires and rushed to follow him, whirling the smoking mares'-tails of flame above their heads. The dead fell thick, and the living, led by Hector, plunged up over the clotted mounds of bodies to come aboard the ships, where on the decks the desperate Greeks still stood to hurl them back.

Still the Trojan tide roared on, past the foremost galleys, while Ajax, shouting to his comrades, "Come on! Come against Hector! This is no dance he makes between our ships!" leapt from deck to deck like a man who drives four horses abreast and leaps from the back of one to the back of another, thrusting all the while with a sea-pike as long as three tall men.

Smoke began to rise, and there was a crackle of flames from old salty ships' timbers, and all the while, above the tumult, rose Hector's trumpet shout, "Fire! Fire the black ships!"

It was then that Patroclus, coming out from the hut of Eurypolus in the furthest part of the camp and upwind of the fighting, saw, as it seemed, half the fleet in flames and the battle whirlpooling around the ships.

1994

Gregory Rogers
Way Home

Gregory Rogers's illustrations are strongly influenced by cinematography. Each double-page spread appears like a frame of film capturing the pace and movement of this story about Shane, a young boy living on the harsh city streets, who finds a lost kitten and protects it in the warmth of his jacket. Through this simple act he discovers a friendship that starkly contrasts with the overt hostility around him.

The dark and forbidding illustrations are placed on a black background and there is a striking rip down each page revealing the different aspects of Shane's world. The rip directs the reader down rubbish-filled back streets and alleys as Shane is chased across the city by a threatening gang. The artist cleverly positions the reader on each page and controls what can be seen in each cinematic frame. Texture, light and shadow are used to stunning effect to capture the mood, danger and fast-moving pace of life on the streets.

Close-up shots reveal Shane's dirty clothes, worn out trainers and unwashed hands, as well as the palpable fear and tension in his arms and legs. Long shots chart his dangerous journey across the city and position him against the bright lights, warmth and wealth of houses, car showrooms and restaurants. The crumpled end-papers and dramatically ripped pages reinforce this notion that Shane is uncared for, worthless and discarded.

This is an emotionally-affecting picture book with sophisticated and thought-provoking illustrations that raise awareness of a serious issue while telling a moving story.

Libby Hathorn
Way Home
Illustrated by Gregory Rogers
Andersen Press, 1994

1995

P J Lynch
The Christmas Miracle of Jonathan Toomey

P J Lynch, already the holder of the Mother Goose Award for most promising newcomer to children's book illustration, was awarded his first Kate Greenaway Medal for the beautifully rich and moving illustrations in this Christmas tale about a lonely, widowed wood-carver whose cold heart is thawed when a widow and her son ask him to carve a set of nativity figures for them.

P J Lynch's detailed, layered watercolour paintings complement the gentle story. The few exterior views, with their closely observed period buildings and wide viewpoints, establish the setting as a small, nineteenth-century New England town. The main part of the story takes place inside Jonathan Toomey's cabin and workshop. The artist draws the reader inside to observe Jonathan's craftsmanship and his transformation by means of a series of beautifully painted interior views, full of the deep brown and golden hues of the wood he carves. The faces and carvings lit by fires and lamps and the convincing textured details of tools and furniture all work to convey a strong sense of place and provide insight into character.

Composition and the use of space are very effective, as text and small motifs are placed to the left of the page, leaving most of the double-page spread for large illustrations. This draws the reader right into the setting and story. Illuminated windows, open doors and a blazing fire give an atmosphere of hope; the way the human figures draw closer together, as in the illustration of Jonathan guiding Thomas's carving, is reflected by the carved figures in a deeply moving way.

The greatest skill of these illustrations lies in the depth of character and feeling they manage to convey. P J Lynch's hours of people-watching from his Dublin studio have been used to good effect. Jonathan Toomey is drawn and painted in a believable and sympathetic way. Those illustrations which focus on Jonathan's face as he sits smoking his pipe, thinking of his dead family are full of emotion and honesty. They make the happy ending of the story, with its themes of love and connection, completely satisfying.

Susan Wojciechowski

The Christmas Miracle of Jonathan Toomey

Illustrated by P J Lynch

Walker Books, 1995

1996

Helen Cooper
The Baby Who Wouldn't Go To Bed

The imaginative world of childhood is the theme for Helen Cooper's picture book about a baby who wants to stay up all night. As the baby plays in his toy car, his bedroom is transformed into a surreal landscape towering with fantasy castles, musical instruments and over-sized toys. Throughout the book there are strong images and references to bedtime routines: the toy soldiers all march with toothbrushes rather than their usual rifles and the little train carries a cast of sleeping nursery rhyme and storybook characters back to the depot. An image of a bed also appears in some of the landscapes, constantly emphasising that sleep is just around the corner. All of the toys and landscapes in the baby's night-time adventure are found in their rightful places in the final double-page spread of the sleeping baby and his mother.

The illustrations are sequenced like a film giving pace and rhythm to the story. Close-ups and long-shots are used to accentuate the madcap sense of scale and perspective of the fantasy world. The small child looks up at a sphinx-like tiger on one page and is viewed from above as he balances on a ladder and speaks to moon on another. Colour and light are used well to create mood and feeling in these changing scenes. Rich yellow and orange tones give a sense of comfort and security to the early, more playful, landscapes while pale, translucent colours are increasingly used as the baby approaches sleep. The artwork is soft yet sparkling; mottled and marbled backgrounds created using layers of watercolour add to this effect and give the book texture and, above all, a real feeling of the warmth and safety of a loving family.

Helen Cooper

The Baby Who Wouldn't Go To Bed

Doubleday, 1996

1997

P J Lynch
When Jessie Came Across the Sea

Irish illustrator, P J Lynch, was awarded the Kate Greenaway Medal for the second time for his illustrations in **When Jessie Came Across the Sea**, a moving story of a Jewish orphan from Eastern Europe who bravely travels to America to begin a new life.

Set at the turn of the nineteenth century, this involving story presents the demanding journey taken by so many emigrants to America in a fairytale style. P J Lynch's illustrations perfectly match the storytelling, while also filling the pages with believable settings, authentic period details and emotionally truthful character studies that ground the story in real experience.

The detailed watercolour illustrations chart the changing settings of Jessie's journey. The contained world of her Eastern European village is depicted in soft green tones with warmly lit interiors which highlight the loving closeness between Jessie and her grandmother. The shipboard scenes are painted in subdued colours and show an excellent use of composition as passengers move from isolation and loneliness to friendship. As America approaches, the delicate watercolour skies appear larger and brighter and facial expressions show a believable mix of hope, determination, uncertainty and fear.

The illustrations of life on the Lower East Side of New York are closely observed. They are filled with fascinating period details and cleverly use space and the placement of text to move the narrative forward and reveal scenes through Jessie's eyes. As Jessie grows up emotionally and physically, the city settings are carefully chosen to present an expanding world for her character. Family scenes and reunions are moving; Jessie's loving nature shines out from the pages as the illustrator draws the reader into the story to provoke a strong emotional reaction.

Amy Hest

When Jessie Came Across the Sea

Illustrated by P J Lynch

Walker Books, 1997

1998

Helen Cooper
Pumpkin Soup

Helen Cooper won her second Kate Greenaway Medal for this humorous and thoughtful look at friendship and sharing, in which a trio of friends – Cat, Duck and Squirrel – quarrel, suffer and make up again when Duck begins to assert his independence over the making of pumpkin soup.

Colour, shape and composition are used to draw the reader closer into a story of domestic drama and tense sibling rivalry. A visit by the illustrator to New England was the inspiration for the pumpkin theme, the forest setting and the depiction of such quintessentially American details as the letter box and the soup kitchen signs. Helen Cooper's illustrations are executed in mixed water-based media and her use of warm orange, red and brown tones perfectly creates the atmosphere of a New England autumn. The recurrence of round shapes throughout the book, such as the pumpkins, bowl and soup pot, has a predominately comforting and reassuring effect.

The cinematic narrative sequence of the illustrations is carefully structured. The opening pages take the reader from a subtly coloured night-time exterior view of the cosy cabin, to a slanted close-up of the window with its harmonious scene of happy soup making, and then even closer into the cabin bedroom with its unsettling shadows and worryingly wide awake Duck. Page space is used to good effect. There are full-page illustrations with detailed settings and close-up views of characters and white pages of text with small illustrations forming action sequences in the style of animation. The use of speech bubbles, exclamations and frames around those illustrations that depict Duck's imagined fates continue the animation effect.

The interactions between the three main characters and the small-scale action sequences are very funny and full of enjoyable effects: for instance, the splashes of pumpkin soup all over the pages. The multi-layered pictures are full of tantalising details waiting to be discovered: pumpkins can be found everywhere; chairs have carved animal heads; the bagpipe tassel is shaped like a cat; and tiny bugs watch the action from a distance.

Helen Cooper

Pumpkin Soup

Doubleday, 1988

1999

Helen Oxenbury
Alice's Adventures in Wonderland

Thirty years after winning her first Kate Greenaway Medal, Helen Oxenbury successfully modernised Lewis Carroll's *Alice's Adventures in Wonderland* to win the award for the second time. In Helen Oxenbury's hands, Alice is a child of today: casually dressed, personable, mischievous and charmingly curious. Her spirit is perfectly captured: she's drawn with a hand on her hip and a defiant gait as she meets the Queen of Hearts and is given a furtive look as she eyes a plateful of jam tarts.

The logic and lunacy of Wonderland is depicted in a series of soft pencil drawings and watercolour paintings reproduced on thick cream paper. Full single- and double-page illustrations are combined with detailed pencil vignettes at the start of each chapter. The large colour illustrations are bright with colour giving a real sense of the warm skies and lush grass.

The sense of scale is perfectly achieved with perspective shifting from page to page: a tiny Alice sits slumped against a table leg with a vast expanse of black and white tiled floor in the background; while a giant Alice is crammed into the frame of a double-page spread with her head pushed against the ceiling and her foot stuck up the open fireplace.

A particular strength of Helen Oxenbury's interpretation is the life that she gives to the diverse cast of supporting characters. The Caterpillar, the Gryphon, the Mock Turtle and the Cheshire Cat are each given their own peculiarities and quirky charm. It's the Mad Hatter that most obviously demonstrates the artist's playful sense of humour, since he bears a striking resemblance to David Lloyd, the Chairman of Walker Books.

This abundantly illustrated edition of *Alice's Adventures in Wonderland* is lovingly crafted by an illustrator who captures the spirit and freedom of childhood, bringing Lewis Carroll's classic story to a new readership while retaining all of its original charm.

Lewis Carroll

Alice's Adventures in Wonderland

Illustrated by Helen Oxenbury

Walker Books, 1999

2000

Lauren Child
I Will Not Ever NEVER Eat a Tomato

Lauren Child's off-beat humour and her refreshing illustrative style are evident in this story about Charlie and his fussy-eating sister, Lola who dislikes peas, carrots, potatoes, mushrooms, cauliflower, cabbage and, most definitely, tomatoes.

The illustrations are heavily influenced by the media and draw on visual imagery from film, television, magazines and advertising. Lauren Child makes full use of digital technology to compose collage pictures using photographs of vegetables, vibrant fabrics, patterned wallpapers and large blocks of bright, flat colour. This is particularly strong in the imaginary worlds that Charlie creates for Lola to trick her into eating some of her most hated foods. The very tip of Mount Fuji is made from photographs of harsh grey rock and is surrounded by wispy clouds clearly torn from sheets of textured white paper to resemble piles of mashed potato.

Cartoon-style drawings of Charlie and Lola are superimposed onto these different backgrounds. They are drawn in bold black lines with confident economy and are given fully expressive facial features and a wonderful sense of movement to their bodies. Lola's angled eyes, tight mouth, folded arms and the sharp dashes of fringe drawn across her forehead depict her crossness at being encouraged to change her dietary habits.

There is a strong sense of design throughout the book. Pages of detailed collage are interspersed with double-page spreads filled with a single photographic image, such as a plate of bright green peas or a huge potato. The layout of the text and the differentiated use of fonts are inspired and integral to the illustrations. Text is tucked into cupboards, stuck onto carrots and shaped into waves, giving a sense of pattern and syncopated rhythm to the story. The result is a fresh, vibrant and very modern picture book full of colour and pattern that pulls the reader head-first into a world that is grounded in reality, yet wildly imaginative.

Lauren Child
I Will Not Ever NEVER Eat a Tomato
Orchard Books, 2000

2001

Chris Riddell
Pirate Diary

Starting in 1716, *Pirate Diary* describes the adventures of nine-year-old Jake Carpenter as he discovers the excitement and perils of life on the high seas. Through Jake's eyes the reader explores the ship, meets the colourful crew and learns about mainmasts, topsails and backstaffs. Despite being a fictionalised account, this is a serious history. The ship, costumes, weapons and customs have all been meticulously researched.

The illustrations continue and extend the text; they match the rhythm of the story and appear at those times when the reader most needs the support of a visual representation. There is a huge cross-section of the ship and a small series of sketches showing how the ship's canon is loaded and fired, for example. Historical notes, a glossary and index are illustrated with black and white line drawings and there are also carefully drawn maps and plans vivid with authentic historical detail. It is the large colour illustrations, however, that have the greatest impact. Single- and double-page spreads are full of action: a gang of pirates swing and scramble onto a ship in a frenzied scene filled with drama and movement and the sounds of gunfire.

Chris Riddell's varied use of design captures the different moods and tempos of pirate life. Each character is individually and expressively drawn in the artist's unique caricaturist style, so that the pain on the face of a man being whipped or having his leg amputated by the ship's doctor is palpable. The use of perspective and colour is skilful: the ship's captain towers over the reader and small Jake climbs the towering rigging above an expanse of sapphire-blue sea.

Text and illustration work hand in hand in this book, giving the reader easy access to a wealth of historical information about merchant ships, piracy, the colonies and life in the early eighteenth century.

Richard Platt
Pirate Diary
Illustrated by Chris Riddell
Walker Books, 2001

2002

Bob Graham
Jethro Byrde Fairy Child

Bob Graham reveals his early love of fairy tales and comics in both the theme and style of this gentle, warm and witty picture book. Annabelle, an imaginative and observant child, discovers a fairy family in the unpromising landscape of her cement and weed-filled suburban backyard. She proceeds to spend an enchanting afternoon entertaining, and being entertained by, her new friends. Annabelle's parents cannot see the fairy child, Jethro Byrde, and his family but they play along with their daughter in a very appealing way. In one of the many witty touches, the tapping of Dad's laptop computer keys gives the background rhythm to the fairy music.

The story pays tribute to Annabelle's ability to look closely and Bob Graham rewards this quality in the reader by his skilled use of perspective, scale and detail. The focus moves from a double-page spread of a panoramic cityscape full of detail, to zoom in on the landscape of Annabelle's backyard. The sense of scale required to contrast human and fairy dimensions is perfectly achieved: the perspective shifts constantly, from birds-eye to child's-eye to fairy-eye viewpoints. The closely observed details of Jethro standing on a bottle top, the fairy baby asleep in a cake case and the fairy on Annabelle's finger are a constant delight.

Bob Graham combines full-page illustrations with smaller framed, comic-style pictures and tiny vignettes. The pen and watercolour washes unite the grey and brown tones of an urban landscape with the rainbow-coloured shades of the fairy world which shine through the gaps in fences and fill the sky.

This picture book celebrates family life, the ordinary becoming extraordinary, and the importance of kindness. The blend of warmth, humour, detail and unusual perspective is only to be expected from an illustrator who is quoted as liking the sound of dogs' ears flapping and who feels that the optimum view of guinea pigs is looking up under their chins.

Bob Graham

Jethro Byrde Fairy Child

Walker Books, 2002

2003

Shirley Hughes
Ella's Big Chance

Shirley Hughes won a second Kate Greenaway Medal for her inventive re-telling of the Cinderella story which is given a glamorous 1920s setting and a satisfying twist. Ella, a talented dressmaker with a kind and loving nature, slaves over her sewing machine to make beautiful clothes for her new stepsisters and chooses Buttons rather than the Duke for her happy ending.

This skilfully composed and designed picture book belongs in a sequence of visually adventurous books for older children created by Shirley Hughes. Upright panels of text are carefully placed on the pages to leave plenty of space for large, sumptuous illustrations in gouache and watercolour with flowing pen lines. Each text panel also contains small black and white line drawings which give the reader more information about plot and character. The use of colour is stunning. The ballroom scenes shimmer with reflected light; the fabrics glow and sparkle; and the scene where Ella and Buttons dance by moonlight is lit with deep blue tones and a skilled use of line and hatching to create shadow effects.

Shirley Hughes's attention to period detail is consummate. The ballroom scenes have a glittering Art Deco style, the dance sequences are inspired by the films of Fred Astaire and Ginger Rogers, and the costumes designed by the artist pay tribute to Doucet, Poiret, Patou and other French couturiers of the 1920s and reflect Shirley Hughes's early study of costume design at Liverpool Art School. This is an atmospheric, graceful picture book with flowing lines that lead the reader through the narrative. The sense of movement is beautifully conveyed throughout: for instance, the bike wobbles convincingly as Buttons, Ella and the cat ride away, laughing, at the end.

Artistry, craftsmanship, imagination and a lightness of touch combine in these illustrations; but, for all its technical brilliance, what the reader will most remember is the loving kindness of the central character and the warm nature of the story. This Cinderella chooses a life of love, work and laughter and the happy-ever-after ending is a convincing one.

Shirley Hughes
Ella's Big Chance
The Bodley Head, 2003

2004

Chris Riddell
Jonathan Swift's Gulliver

Chris Riddell's illustrations bring to life the people, creatures and kingdoms of Swift's searing imagination in this re-telling of Gulliver's four voyages to Lilliput, Brobdingnag, Laputa and finally to the land of the Houyhnhnms, where horses rule over humans. It's a beautifully designed book. The illustrations are comic and often surreal. There are huge double-page spreads of intense colour, supplemented by smaller black and white line drawings. They are executed with attention to detail and complete control over scale and perspective. Each spread is a little episode that can be read on its own, making this complex story, originally written as a satire on Whig and Tory politics in the early eighteenth century, highly accessible and entertaining for a new audience of young readers.

Chris Riddell gives each land Gulliver visits its own idiom. The tiny Lilliputians are pantomime fools dressed in spotted knickerbockers, bows, ruffles and mismatched shoes with oversized moustaches, pointed noses and ridiculous hairstyles. An egg motif, symbolic of the two warring factions in Lilliputian society, dominates the costumes and architecture and adds to the peculiarity of the land and its people. The rather more admirable Brobdignagians are depicted as oriental giants and this time there are subtle elements of blue and white chinoiserie flowing through the illustrations. The effects of scale are nicely realised with the now tiny Gulliver struggling to drink from an egg-cup the size of a bucket and half drowning in a huge bowl of cream.

The artist's skills as a political cartoonist are evident in the illustrations of Gulliver's third voyage to the floating island of Laputa and his encounter with the Academy, where various mad professors are busy extracting sunshine from cucumbers and turning ice into gunpowder. In Chris Riddell's hands, though, the Academy becomes a satire on the aspirations of New Labour, complete with a wonderful caricature of former Prime Minister Tony Blair being prodded and poked by academics to remind him of the political promises he has made.

Martin Jenkins

Jonathan Swift's Gulliver

Illustrated by Chris Riddell

Walker Books, 2004

2005

Emily Gravett
Wolves

Originally a project for Emily Gravett's degree in illustration at Brighton University, **Wolves** went on to win the Macmillan Prize for illustration. A naïve rabbit borrows a book about wolves from the public library and becomes so absorbed in its fascinating information that he fails to notice the wolf right behind him. The library book's vital fact that a wolf's diet includes rabbits alas comes too late.

This beautifully produced book contains mixed-media techniques, pencil drawings and interactive elements such as a library card and letters. The style is spare, but the expert composition and use of cream page space means that the eye is always drawn to the quirky drawings and characters. The witty text is full of rabbit-related puns and is complemented by clever visual jokes: for instance, a pack of wolves burst out of a cardboard box and an urban wolf wears a hoodie. The artist uses a few simple pencil lines to constantly change the position of the rabbit's ears and to create humour and character. Viewpoint changes throughout the rabbit's journey with the pencil-work becoming ever more detailed as the scale increases. The final close-up of the huge wolf's eyes right behind the rabbit has great drama.

The device of making this book turn into the very book that the rabbit is reading is brilliantly done with every detail considered: the texture of the book cover is well achieved; the brown scored endpapers are reproduced in both books; and the chewed book effects are totally convincing. The torn paper technique of the alternative ending and the final double-page spread with its letter-strewn doormat are thought-provoking and interactive. Design and production is exemplary and reflects Emily Gravett's training as a bookbinder, as well as an artist.

Emily Gravett

Wolves

Macmillan, 2005

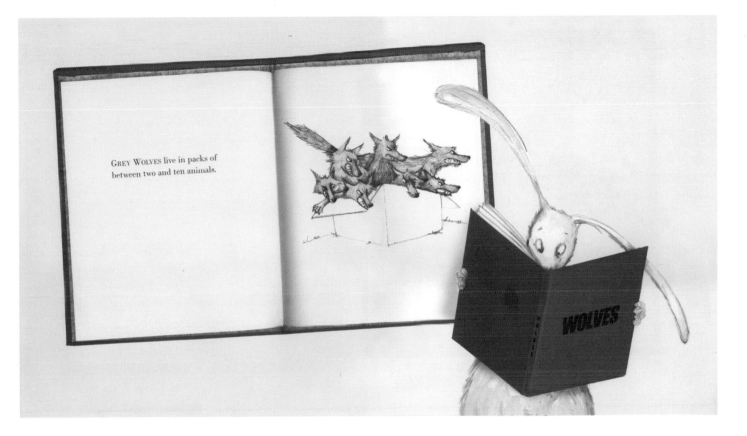

GREY WOLVES live in packs of between two and ten animals.

2007

Mini Grey
The Adventures of the Dish and the Spoon

Mini Grey's picture book combines humour, imagination and originality and plays with a mix of different media to create sophisticated illustrations with a huge visual impact. *The Adventures of the Dish and the Spoon* is an evocative Hollywood re-working of the classic nursery rhyme. The dish and spoon run away, make their fortune, fall on hard times and turn to a life of crime. There are many hard-knocks, scrapes and breaks before, in a truly romantic ending, the couple find love again over the moon.

An exceptional sense of composition and comic-book techniques are used to split the double-page spreads into a series of linked cinematic frames which guide the reader through the story. On some pages a quick succession of frames down the page adds movement, pace and drama to the story. The cinematic theme is continued in the film and other cultural references that occur throughout the book and which clearly set the story in 1930s America. There are nods to westerns, the Keystone Cops and Bonnie and Clyde, as well as references to the toys, costume and architecture of the period.

The illustrations combine collage with watercolour and pastels to bring a freshness and vitality to the story. The dish, the spoon and the wonderful supporting cast of cutlery are all given fully expressive faces using just two eyes. Mini Grey is incredibly skilled at giving character and emotion to inanimate objects. Her kitchen knives are villainous and there is something incredibly touching about the armless spoon placing a bet at the casino and later slumped down in his prison cell. Visual jokes and the little details hidden in the pictures add meaning to the text and bring a wonderful sense of discovery and fun to the book.

Mini Grey

The Adventures of the Dish and the Spoon

Jonathan Cape, 2006

They tried to frighten the Dish. What could we do?

We couldn't pay them back.